The EZ Guide to Aeroponics, Hydroponics & Aquaponics

By Bob Long

Table of Contents

- Chapter 1 -

Introduction

Ponos is the god of labor in Greek mythology and the basis for the Greek word "ponics" which means hard work. In modern English, ponics is combined with the Greek and Latin words for air and water in describing 3 different methods of soil less gardening; hydroponics, aeroponics and aquaponics.

Photosynthesis in plants requires access to minerals, especially nitrogen, phosphorus and potassium. These nutrients are found naturally in the soil but the soil itself is not required for plant growth. So the common thread in all soil less gardening techniques is the existence of an alternative means of delivering the necessary minerals directly to the roots of the plants.

In this book we will cover 3 of the most popular methods of soil less gardening.

1) Hydroponics

Hydro is the Greek word for water and Hydroponics literally means "working water." It is the name for the process of growing plants in beds of sand, gravel, or similar supporting material that is flooded with nutrient rich water based solutions. Hydroponics goes back 1000s of years to the early Egyptians, Aztecs and Chinese and one of the 7 wonders of the ancient world, the Hanging Gardens of Babylon, is thought to be an early application of hydroponic cultivation. Hydroponics is the simplest and most fool proof of the three systems to implement but also the least efficient. Regardless it enables easy indoor gardening and will typically produce crops on less land while using only 10% of the water that is required for traditional agriculture.

2) Aeroponics

Aero is the Greek word for air and aeroponics is a gardening technique that grows plants without anchoring them in soil or the aggregate media that is used in hydroponics. In aeroponics, the plants' roots are suspended in air in a chamber and intermittently spayed or misted with nutrient-laden water. The goal is to hold the humidity of the chamber at or close to 100% which exposes the roots to abundant oxygen and CO_2 as well as precisely measured levels of the required nutrients. Aeroponics is a relatively new high tech method of gardening dating back to the end of the 20th century. It is well suited to indoor gardening and can produce crop yields that exceed hydroponics by as much as 40%. It is also more complicated and less forgiving then hydroponics. The wet/dry spray cycles must be consistently timed and crops can be severely damaged or completely lost due to even short electrical power outages or equipment failures.

3) Aquaponics

Aqua is the Latin word for water and aquaponics is the modern practice of growing fish and plants in a closed water system utilizing the natural synergistic relationship between these two species. Aquaponics combines hydroponics with aquaculture to create a sustainable food producing process that regularly yields organic fruits or vegetables and healthy fish populations for either consumption or as ornamental pets. Aquaculture or fish farming is the growing of aquatic species, such as fish, crayfish and prawns in a controlled environment. As stated, hydroponics is growing plants in a solution of water and nutrients.

As they eat and grow fish produce waste that introduce ammonia into the water which is toxic to most aquatic animals. Through a natural multi-step process known as the Nitrogen Cycle, ammonia from fish waste products are transformed by bacteria into nitrates that are a source of the nutrients that are needed by plants. The plants feed on these nutrients and filter and clean the water for the fish. By combining these two systems, aquaponics is the ideal answer to a fish farmer's problem of maintaining water quality and a hydroponic grower's need for nutrient rich water.

All three of these growing methods can be used for indoor, soil less food production year around. They provide an alternative for would be urban gardeners who lack outdoor space and a potential means for full scale food production in areas of the world with limited access to arable land.

Chapter 2

What is Hydroponics?

Hydroponics is derived from the Greek words Hydro meaning water and Ponics meaning work. It literally means "working water" and is a method of growing plants without soil by submersing their roots in water based nutrient solutions. Hydroponics goes back 1000s of years to the early civilizations of the Egyptians, Aztecs and Babylonians. The Hanging Gardens of Babylon, which is one of the seven wonders of the ancient world, is thought to be an early example of hydroponics.

Today hydroponics is increasingly used to address hunger by providing a stable food supply for locations with limited or no access to arable land. It is also used by urban gardeners who want to grow fresh fruit and vegetables indoors or on their roof tops. It is even being experimented with by NASA to provide a sustainable food supply for deep space travel or future colonies on the Moon or Mars.

Photosynthesis in plants requires access to minerals, especially nitrogen, phosphorus and potassium. These nutrients are found naturally in the soil but the soil itself is not required for plant growth. So in the simplest sense hydroponics is about alternative methods of delivering those minerals to the roots of plants directly without soil.

There are several different approaches to delivery but the common element is a water based solution with a proper mixture of the necessary nutrients. By directly applying this solution to the roots, hydroponics is an efficient growing process that can produce crops on about 20% of the land while using only 10% of the water as traditional soil based agriculture. Crops are able to be planted in close proximity to each other and also vertically on elevated trays saving space while the water is conserved since it is recycled. By eliminating soil you also eliminate all soil born diseases and significantly reduce the need for pesticides

 In all the various forms of hydroponics, the plants roots are immersed in carefully measured water based nutrient solution. The dissolved minerals are delivered to the roots through several techniques which include continuous water flow, various floods and drain concepts, and the use of misters and sprayers in a hydroponics' derivative method called Aeroponics.

Virtually any plant can be grown utilizing hydroponics, but some plants are more suitable than others. Lettuce, tomatoes, cucumbers, peppers and most herbs are some of the best choices for hydroponic gardeners. With hydroponics these plants can be grown indoors and harvests can take place year round. For anybody living in a location with limited or no access to arable land, hydroponics is an effective alternative for producing a stable supply of fresh fruit and vegetables.

Chapter 3

Types of Hydroponic Systems

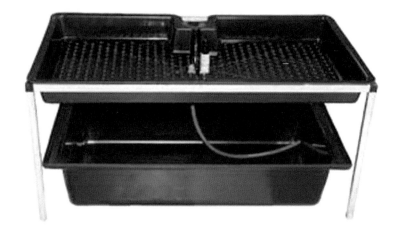

There are 4 basic types of hydroponic systems, that will be covered in this chapter; Deep Water Culture (DWC), Ebb and Flow (Flood & Drain), Drip Systems and N.F.T. (Nutrient Film Technique). There are also different variations of these basic systems, but all hydroponic methods are derived from these four. Aeroponics will be addressed separately in its own section of this book.

Deep Water Culture (DWC)

The deep water culture system is the simplest of all active hydroponic systems. This design can be constructed using household items as simple as a bucket, an old aquarium or almost any water tight container. A cover for the bucket with a hole(s) or a Styrofoam platform floating on the nutrient solution can be used to hold the plants in place allowing the roots to dip into the liquid. The plants are first secured in permeable pots that are filled with aggregate material and then inserted in the holes in the cover or Styrofoam. Net pots are the standard commercial device for holding the plants but simple plastic cups with drilled holes will work too. A pump connected to an air stone supply bubbles that stir the solution and provide oxygen to the roots of the plants. Illustrations of DWC systems are shown below.

Deep Water Culture systems are excellent for growing lettuce which is a fast growing water loving plant. Herbs and small flowers also do well in DWC systems. The DWC design is vulnerable to root rot so larger and slower growing plants do not do as well.

Spacing between net pots in multi plant set ups can vary based on the type and size of plant but standard spacing of 8 inches or 20 cm is a good starting point. Rockwool is the best aggregate material to use in the net pots though less expensive gravel will also work.

Because of its simple design, the DWC hydroponic system is a good choice for homemade hydroponic systems. Besides being one of the easiest and cheapest to build and setup, it is requires little maintenance, and has very few moving parts that can fail.

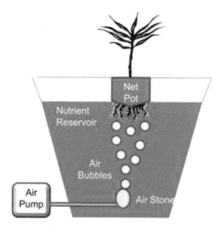

Deep Water Culture System

DWC Bucket Cover with Net pots

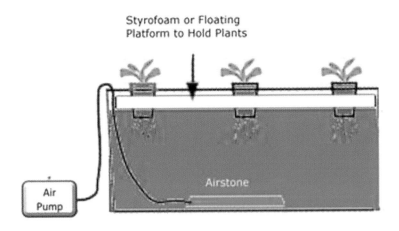

Styrofoam or Floating
Platform to Hold Plants

Air
Pump

Airstone

Multi-Plant DWC System

EBB & FLOW - (FLOOD AND DRAIN)

The Ebb and Flow system has a container commonly called a grow tray to hold the plants and a separate tank or reservoir for the nutrient solution. The system operates by utilizing a pump connected to a timer to temporarily flood the grow tray with nutrients and then gravity drains the liquid back into the reservoir.

When the timer turns the pump on, nutrient solution is pumped into the grow tray filling it up to an overflow point which should be set at about 80% of the height of the media in the tray. When the timer shuts the pump off the nutrient solution flows back into the reservoir through a fill/drain valve and then the pump. Most pumps will have a rating called "HEAD" which is a measure of how high it will lift the nutrient solution. To ensure the proper stream of nutrients (neither too strong nor weak) you will want a pump with a HEAD rating of about twice the height that you need to propel the water (from the top of the pump to the top of the overflow valve).

The timing of flood and drain cycles is dependent on many factors including the size of the tanks, capacity of the pump, the ambient temperature, humidity, the type of aggregate being used (Rockwool retains moisture much longer than gravel for example) and the type of plants that are being grown. We recommend starting with four 15 minute flood cycles per day and watch how the plants respond and then adjust accordingly. You should try to fill the tank to the overflow point each cycle so for smaller pumps the on time may be longer but do not keep the roots submerged underwater for more than 1 hour. As the roots grow bigger more water should be applied by either adding cycles or increasing the length of the flood phase.

Ebb & Flow can use a variety of growing mediums to either fill the entire tray or in individual net pots that are then placed in the tray with the plants. The main disadvantage of this type of system is that pump failures or power outages that interrupt the watering cycles can cause the roots to dry out quickly damaging or killing the plants. For this reason Rockwool is the preferred aggregate material for Ebb & Flow since it retains more moisture but gravel, perlite, clay pellets or grow rocks are all workable alternatives.

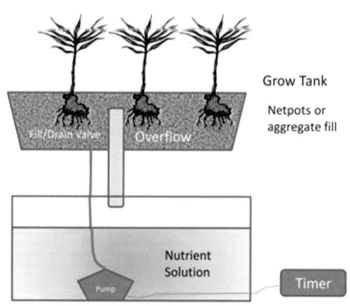

Ebb & Flow Hydroponics System

Ebb & Flow Hydroponics Systems can grow most plants that can be grown in a garden but water loving plants with short roots do the best. Some favorites are lettuce, spring onions and herbs.

DRIP SYSTEMS

Drip systems are configured similarly to Ebb & Flow systems with a pump delivering the nutrient solution and gravity draining it from the grow tray. The big difference is instead of flooding the grow tank in short cycles drip emitters are used to slowly deliver nutrients to the roots over much longer time periods. Drip systems can be left on continuously or turned on and off with a timer. When the pump is on nutrient solution is dripped onto the base of each plant by a small drip line. The timing of the cycles is variable based on the same outside factors as the Ebb & Flow system plus the type of drip emitters that are being used. It should be similar to what would be used for the same plants being grown in a traditional garden with a drip irrigation system. We suggest starting with at least 8 hours on per day. The best timing for a drip hydroponics system will never totally submerge the roots while also never allowing them to completely dry out.

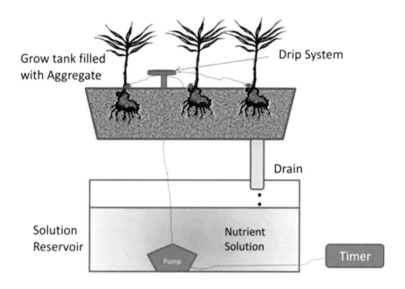

Drip Hydroponics Systems

The biggest drawback with drip systems is clogging of the emitters. Organic nutrients are full of particles and for this reason should be avoided when using a drip system.

N.F.T. (Nutrient Film Technique)

NFT is a very productive method of growing plants by providing a highly oxygenated, slowly moving stream of nutrients to the roots of plants grown in a shallow grow tray. One end of the container is lower than the other to enable the nutrient solution to flow to a drain where it is returned to the reservoir. N.F.T. systems have a constant flow of nutrient solution so a timer is not required for the submersible pump.

Plants are spaced in net pots at intervals along the growing box with their root ends dangling into and constantly moistened by the nutrient film. There is usually no growing medium and the flow is shallow enough to expose much of the root mass directly to oxygen.

N.F.T. systems are highly efficient and can result in explosive growth, but are also very susceptible to power outages and pump failures. The roots dry out very rapidly when the flow of nutrient solution is interrupted. Another drawback with this method of hydroponic gardening is that the plants must have a root system large enough to hang down into the nutrient solution.

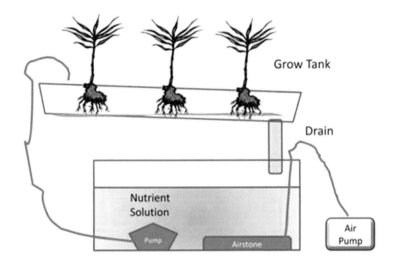

N.F.T. System

N.F.T. systems are not the best choice for beginners.

Chapter 4

What is Aeroponics?

Many practitioners consider aeroponics just another branch of hydroponics like Ebb & Flow or N.F.T. since it essentially grows plants using a soil less solution of water and nutrients. However as a relatively new, high tech method, I think aeroponics is sufficiently distinct from hydroponics to merit its own section in this book.

Like hydroponics, aeroponics provides a fast, clean and efficient approach to food production. Crops can be planted indoors without soil and can be harvested year round. However in aeroponics, plants are grown in chambers with their roots suspended in space and periodically bathed in a nutrient mist. In hydroponics the plants are usually anchored by their roots in a "grow media" and doused with nutrient enriched water. By further exposing the plants roots to oxygen, aeroponics can produce dramatic improvements in yields over other gardening methods. Aeroponics is increasingly being used for a wide range of purposes from greenhouse cloning of plants, to NASA growing food for long distance space flights, to individuals legally cultivating medical marijuana in some states and not so legally in others.

Advantages of Aeroponics

Many people are unaware of the role that oxygen plays in photosynthesis and plant growth. Traditional gardening methods and hydroponics which bury the roots in soil or grow media restrict access to oxygen which is a limiting factor on growth. In aeroponics systems, the plants are secured by a flexible collar and the roots are exposed in an open space so there is plenty of oxygen to be absorbed along with the nutrients. That is one reason that for a given space, aeroponics systems are typically able to produce up to 80% more fruit and vegetables than traditional gardens and 40% greater than standard hydroponics. Aeroponics systems use considerably less water and chemicals than traditional agriculture with reports of savings exceeding 90% in water usage, fertilizer and pesticides. Aeroponics systems can be used to clone the best specimens in a garden by rapidly rooting cuttings for replanting. They can more efficiently germinate seeds or grow plants from seed to harvest. Using aeroponics systems as part of a replanting program improves root growth, survival rate, and maturation time. Urban gardeners where soil is often scarce or unavailable have found that aeroponics systems suit their needs well by enabling them to grow produce inside their apartments or on their rooftops. It is also a valuable alternative for rural locations where arable soil is scarce or the water supply limited.

Disadvantages of Aeroponics

Aeroponics systems are not easy to set up or operate and are not the perfect solution to all gardening problems. The setup costs are high and to be successful in aeroponics requires precise control of nutrients and water.

It is more temperamental than traditional gardening or hydroponics since pH changes and nutrient imbalances adversely impact plants much more quickly due to increased absorption rates and the high level of oxygenation. These are the same factors that enable the rapid growth of the plants in a properly balanced system.

Aeroponics depends almost entirely on high-pressure pumps, timers and sprayers, so power failures and equipment malfunctions can have a devastating effect. Electrical outages can be mitigated through backup generators or a computer UPS, but those solutions add to the cost. If the system has a pump failure, bad nutrients, dry reservoir or blocked nozzles, the plants can be badly damaged or killed in just a few hours.

Current State of Aeroponics

While the practice of hydroponics has been around for thousands of years, aeroponics is a relatively new development that was first developed during the last decades of the 20th century. The technology behind aeroponics systems is still evolving and it is a more complicated process than hydroponics or conventional gardening. Aeroponics in its different forms is a high-tech growing method that requires expertise, investment, and monitoring. It is growing as a hobby for indoor gardeners and also commercially as an efficient means of propagation and germination. Because of the increased absorption rates of nutrients and oxygen, aeroponics in the hands of a well experienced gardener can yield explosive and unprecedented growth rates.

Chapter 5

Alternative Aeroponics Designs

Aeroponics is still developing and there are several different designs that are commercially available. In addition, if you are moderately skilled, at do it yourself projects it is also possible to build a DIY Aeroponics system with materials that can be found at most hardware stores. The common element in these alternatives is the predominant exposure of the plant's root system to air.

True Aeroponics

In true aeroponics, pumps controlled by a short cycle timer deliver water and nutrients to the roots through sprayers or misters. The roots hang in the air and are moistened with an oxygen rich hydroponic nutrient solution for roughly five seconds every 20 minutes. This cycle varies by the crop that is being grown. This keeps the roots moist while providing a maximum amount of oxygen. In true aeroponics, the plant's roots are also allowed to fully drain while still in a humid, dark environment. This enables the roots to absorb more nutrients without burning than in hydroponics or traditional gardening. This system requires the precise application of nutrients and the correct timing of wet and dry cycles. There are 2 approaches to true aeroponics:

 Low pressure systems use nozzles similar to a sprinkler system to spray nutrients directly on the roots. These spray nozzles are connected by PVC pipes.

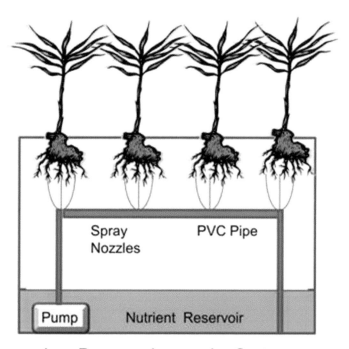

Low Pressure Aeroponics System

High pressure systems use a fogger/atomizer that reduces the size of the droplets of solution to a fine mist. This is similar to the misters that you may see used to cool off patrons at outdoor summer events or to keep fruit and vegetables moist at a produce stand.

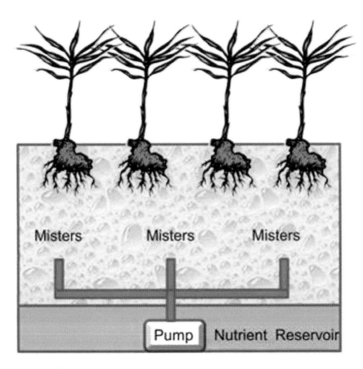

High Pressure Aeroponics System

High pressure systems are more expensive but provide better distribution of nutrients avoiding potential dry spots on the roots as they grow. The drawbacks of true aeroponics is that in the event of a power outage or equipment failure the plants can be severely damaged or die within several hours. In addition, very high quality nutrient solutions must be used to avoid clogging the sprayer heads. True aeroponics can handle the largest plants and provide the best growth rates but also require the most expertise and are far less forgiving then any of the hydroponic designs.

Deep Flow Aeroponics

Deep Flow aeroponics is a hybrid of the aeroponics and hydroponics methods. The system is aeroponics because it uses misters or sprayers to oxygenate and distribute the nutrients and hydroponics because the grow chamber is configured to prevent all the nutrients from draining so as with a N.F.T. design at least a portion of the roots are always submerged. Systems of this type typically hold about one inch of nutrient in the grow chamber. The advantage of this design is that there is a buffer in the event of a power outage or equipment malfunction. This "insurance" against potential failures comes at the cost of slower growth and more incidences of root rot and pathogens that are not generally experienced in true aeroponics.

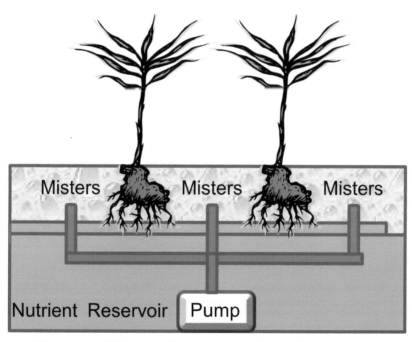

Deep Flow Aeroponics System

Chapter 6

DIY Aeroponics

You can build aeroponics systems out of supplies that are readily available at garden centers and hardware stores. Here is how to build a simple low pressure DIY aeroponics system. We are sticking with a low pressure design rather than a high pressure system, since the precision required in the construction is more forgiving and the materials less expensive. If you want a high pressure system, which provides the most control over the process and produces the highest yields, we suggested buying a commercial unit or kit. For most people a low pressure system is adequate and will still produce a significant improvement over traditional gardening in terms of yield and time to market.

First you need a container with a lid. This can be a bucket, a tote or just about anything that is strong enough to hold the nutrient solution and with a large enough surface area to contain the number and size of plants that you want to grow. The container must be constructed from opaque material since roots are genetically conditioned to grow in dark spaces. The material is also something that you will want to be able to easily drill and cut holes into so a dark plastic is a good choice. Notch the top rim of the container to hold the power cord from the pump that will be used to drive the system. You will also need smaller container(s) that can be filled with media to hold the plants. This can be net pots that you can purchase or something as simple as plastic cups with holes drilled in the bottom to allow the roots to pass through into the main container.

The holes you cut in the lid should match the circumference of the cups or net pots so that they fit but do not fall through the lid. You can select smaller containers to grow a greater number of small plants or larger ones for fewer large plants. For simplicity, we will use growth media to anchor the plants in place in the net pots. There is a wide range of inert materials which can be used for this purpose. Heydite, clay pellets, perlite, vermiculite, and rockwool are the most popular choices. The media that works best are pH neutral, provide support for the plants while exposing as much of the root system to the open air in the chamber as possible.

Clay Pellets   **Perlite**   **Rockwool**

You will need a riser, a 360 degree spray head, and a water pump. For larger systems with multiple spray heads you will also need PVC pipe. This is all standard plumbing and irrigation components and can be found in any hardware store. Place the pump in the bottom of the bucket and cut the riser so that when you mount the spray head it is close to the bottom of the net pot. The pump should drive enough water to completely soak the roots contained in the net pot.

Riser   360 Spray Heads   Multiple Spray Heads

Get a multi cycle timer, preferably a short cycle timer, and program it to run the pump alternating wet and dry cycles. The wet cycle should run long enough to soak the roots and then the dry cycle long enough to allow the solution to drain back into the container. You need to experiment with the timing of these cycles since it is dependent on the strength of the pump, the size and number of net pots and type of timer you have. You want to maintain humidity in the container as close to 100% as possible. Ideally, the roots should never be more than damp nor allowed to become overly dry and very short cycles are preferred. A typical cycle would be 5 seconds on followed by 5 minutes off.

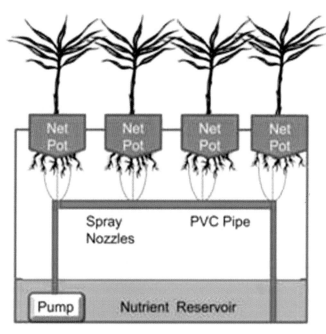

Low Pressure Aeroponics System

- Chapter 7 –

Aeroponics in Outer Space

Aeroponics provides a clean, efficient, and rapid method of food production. Crops can be planted without soil and harvested year-round. In aeroponics, plants roots are suspended in air, periodically sprayed with a nutrient rich water based solution and then allowed to drain. By alternating wet and dry cycles, the roots are kept moist but also exposed to an abundant supply of oxygen leading to much faster growth than traditional gardening methods. Aeroponics systems reduce water and fertilizer usage by over 90% and by avoiding exposure to soil-born diseases eliminate pesticide usage altogether.

These benefits, along with the great reduction in weight that is achieved by eliminating dirt and significantly reducing the amount of water required for plant growth, are reasons this high-tech method of food production has attracted the interest and support of NASA. One of the hurdles to be cleared for long distance space travel and colonies on the Moon or nearby planets is finding a means for crews to manage self- sustaining supplies of food and oxygen.

Through aeroponics, this goal becomes a realistic possibility and humans and plants can become best friends in deep space. Humans consume oxygen and release carbon dioxide. Plants return the favor by consuming carbon dioxide and releasing oxygen. Humans can use edible parts of plants for nourishment, while human waste and inedible plant matter can be re-cycled into the nutrient solution used in aeroponics for plant growth. The plants consume the nutrients and return clean water to the system. So aeroponics is a potential source of food, fresh oxygen, and clean drinking water and together with humans can create a closed and self-sustaining ecological system.

While aeroponics has not yet been used in long distance space travel, like many other aspects of NASA's technological research, spin-off designs are now being used in commercial agricultural applications for food production. This technology is used to relieve hunger in parts of the world with limited access to arable land and to enable city dwellers to grow their own supply of fresh fruits and vegetables. Aeroponics has also led to advances in cloning of plants from cuttings. Numerous plants which were previously considered difficult, or impossible, to propagate from cuttings can now be replicated simply from a single stem. This is a boon to green houses attempting to propagate their best specimens. With a basic aeroponics setup, any interested individual can now clone plants. Finally, crops can also be grown in half the time required by traditional agricultural methods and require far less labor to harvest.

Floating Zucchini in Zero Gravity

Whether in outer space or on Earth, aeroponics has the potential to become an enabling technology in providing the essentials for human life.

Chapter 8

Nutrient Solutions

No matter which hydroponics or aeroponics design you decide on, there is one factor common to them all--- a nutrient solution. This liquid fertilizer must contain all the nutrients your plants need, in a readily absorbed form, delivered right to the root zone of the plant. Properly done this will create optimum growing conditions resulting in fast growing crops of delicious and healthy produce. There are 3 factors to consider in determining the quality of the nutrients that you add to your plants.

First the nutrient concentrate is mixed with water from your home and you need to know whether you have hard or soft water. Soft water which has a low mineral content is preferable. Hard water has lots of mineral content and calcium carbonate in particular. If you test your water through either a test kit or your local health department, calcium content above 70 PPM is considered hard water. There are specific nutrient solutions that are designed to work with hard water as long as the mineral content is below 300 PPM. However, you cannot use water that has gone through a water softener system for hydroponics since it is too salty. If you have really poor quality water that is above 300 PPM, you should consider installing a reverse osmosis filter. These devices typically cost $150 - $300 and have the side benefit of significantly improving the taste of your drinking water while making it usable for hydroponics.

Second is ph, which simply is a number that tells how acidic or alkaline a liquid solution is. The target range of ph for hydroponics is between 5.5 and 6.5 with 6.0 ideal. When the ph is outside this range, the plants cannot access the nutrients. A PH of 7.0 is neutral so hydroponics works best with slightly acidic water. Test kits for ph are inexpensive and readily available in the form of drops or strips. These kits are easy to understand and commonly used to test the ph in swimming pools or aquariums. There are also "ph up/down" chemicals that can be used to correct the level in a nutrient solution that is outside the bounds of the required range. As an alternative you can use muriatic acid or white vinegar to bring PH down or baking soda to raise it. It is a good idea to test for PH at least once a week until you get a better sense for the stability of the solution in your particular hydroponics set up.

Finally, since you are taking soil away from the plant, the nutrient solution you provide as an alternative must be balanced and complete. Plants need large amounts of 6 nutrients; Nitrogen, Phosphorus, Potassium, Calcium, Sulfur and Magnesium. Plants also need minute traces of iron, boron, manganese, zinc, molybdenum, copper, cobalt, chlorine, selenium and silicon in order to thrive. When starting out we strongly suggest buying one of the commercial nutrient solutions that are available at most garden centers or online as opposed to trying to mix your own. In the best commercial solutions all 6 major minerals plus the trace elements are provided in the proper ratio. Only buy solutions formulated specifically for hydroponics. Regular fertilizer will kill your soil less garden.

There are a dizzying number brands that are available but stick with the more well known ones and then experiment to see what works best for your plants. Some of the more commonly used brands that can be purchased at garden centers, hydroponics stores or online are:

- Advanced Nutrients

- General Hydroponics

- Dyna-Grow

- Bontanicaire

- Ionic Hydro

Each of these brands contains all the elements that the plant normally would get from the soil and are highly concentrated, using 2 to 4 teaspoons per gallon of water. They often come in liquid or powered mixes to make two solutions, one for growth and one for bloom.

Since the plants consume the nutrients, the solution in the reservoir needs to be periodically replenished. There really isn't a set amount of time that can be used to determine how often you should change your solution but here is a good rule of thumb to follow. You will lose water to evaporation and plant uptake but the strength of the solution does not necessarily drop with the level of the water and often goes up or gets stronger. First, as the level of solution drops, top off the tank with fresh water without adding any nutrients added. Then check and adjust your PH to maintain it between 5.5 and 6.5. Keep a record of how much water you are putting in the reservoir when topping it off and once that amount equals half of the reservoir capacity it is time to change the solution. For example, if you have a 20 gallon reservoir, you should replace the entire solution once you have added 10 gallons. Again, experiment with the timing and watch how the plants react.

- Chapter 9 –

Aeroponics vs. Hydroponics

In urban centers where access to arable land is often limited, prospective gardeners should evaluate the advantages and disadvantages of aeroponics vs. hydroponics as alternative means for growing fresh fruits and vegetables without soil. Both approaches require the careful application of nutrient solutions to the roots of the plants. Both systems will produce much better yields of produce than traditional gardening and most plants that can be grown in backyard gardens can also be grown via one of "ponics."

Aeroponics vs. Hydroponics: Pluses and Minuses

Both hydroponics and aeroponics are more productive than traditional agriculture and can grow more plants faster in less space. Both methods enable plants to be grown indoors, year round, without soil and conserve significant amounts of water. Here are some differences:

Faster Growth and Greater Risk of Failure

Aeroponics is well suited to indoor gardening and can produce crop yields that exceed hydroponics by as much as 40%. Aeroponics is also more complicated and less forgiving then hydroponics. The wet/dry spray cycles must be consistently timed and crops can be severely damaged or completely lost due to relatively brief electrical power outages or equipment failures. Lacking the stabilizing effect of being rooted in media, plants will be react much more quickly to any adverse changes in PH or the chemical composition of the water leaving less leeway to take corrective action.

This is one of several pluses to growing plants in air without the use of an anchoring media. With misters periodically spraying nutrients onto the roots, enclosed aeroponics chambers hold humidity inside effectively watering continuously without the need for an ongoing water flow. With the roots of the plants exposed to open air they receive as much oxygen as needed. When crops are planted in soil or hydroponics media, this pure oxygenation of the root system is restricted and the growth to harvest takes longer.

Cloning

Cloning of plants is also made possible for anyone through the practice of aeroponics. Very fast root development of cuttings enables easy propagation of the best specimens in a nursery. Since each plant is separated and the roots are not anchored in dirt or media, harvesting is simple.

Reduced Risk from Bacteria and Fungus

In aeroponics, the complete separation between plants also saves the crop from potential total destruction due to the spread of a bacteria or fungus. Aeroponics limits disease transmission since plant-to-plant contact is eliminated. In the case of soil or aggregate, disease can spread throughout the growth media, infecting many plants. A unique advantage of aeroponics technology is that if a particular plant does become diseased, it can be quickly removed from the support structure without disrupting or infecting the other plants.

For inexperience gardeners who want to try their hand at soil less cultivation, hydroponics is the safe choice. It can produce very good results with a relatively hands off approach after initial set up. However if you have the attention to detail and time to monitor your system aeroponics will produce superior results.

Chapter 10

What is Aquaponics?

Aquaponics is the emerging practice of growing fish and plants in a closed water system utilizing the natural synergistic relationship between these two species. A wide variety of fish have been raised as either a food source or as pets in backyard tanks and ponds and as with aeroponics and hydroponics, most plants that are grown in the soil in home gardens can also be cultivated in aquaponic grow beds. As with the other two "ponics" there are the many different options that are available for designing and operating an aquaponics system.

Aquaponics, itself, is the combination of aquaculture and hydroponics to create a sustainable and efficient method of food production. Both hydroponics and aquaculture have long histories going back hundreds of years, while aquaponics is a relatively new field with serious research dating back to the 1970's. Nonetheless, many aquaponics enthusiasts around the country have experienced great success creating sustainable aquaponic systems that regularly produce organic fruits or vegetables and healthy fish populations for either consumption or as ornamental pets.

Aquaponics is much more efficient than traditional vegetable gardens and will produce higher crop yields with less cost and effort. With this technique, you hit two birds with one stone: fish thrive in the closed freshwater system and from their waste products produce the nutrients needed by plants, which in turn, by feeding on the nutrients in the system, filter and clean the water for the fish.

Edible fruits and vegetables or ornamental plants can be grown in aquaponics plant beds. Aquaponics fish can be raised as either an additional food source or as pets. Tilapia, bass, crappie, koi and goldfish are all popular choices for aquaponics fish.

Demystifying Aquaponics

Aquaponics is usually defined as a hybrid of two existing methods: aquaculture and hydroponics.

As discussed earlier in this book, hydroponics is a method of growing plants in a solution of water and nutrients, without soil. This solution is created by adding the nutrients that plants need to the water, which are then fed directly to the plant's roots. Hydroponics can be used to provide plants with the ideal water and nutrient ratios and optimum conditions for growth.

Aquaculture, also known as aqua farming, is the growing of aquatic species, such as fish, crayfish and prawns in a controlled environment. A key to success in aquaculture is the ability to grow healthy fish by maintaining water quality through the removal of adverse chemicals produced from fish waste products. Aquaponics combines these methods to produce fresh fruits and vegetables while at the same time sustaining a freshwater fish system.

As they eat and grow aquaponics fish produce waste that introduces ammonia into the water. Even at relatively low concentrations ammonia is toxic to fish. Through a natural process known as the Nitrogen Cycle, ammonia from fish waste products are transformed by beneficial bacteria in the water into nitrites which are subsequently converted again by bacteria into nitrates. While, nitrites are also toxic to fish at low concentrations, nitrates are not. However, high levels of nitrates in water are problematic for fish.

Fortunately, nitrates are composed of the same nutrients that are needed by plants. By consuming these nitrates, the plants filter the water to create a clean and safe environment for the fish. By producing ammonia in the first place, the fish in an aquaponics system provide the nutrients required by the plants.

By combining these two older practices, aquaponics is the ideal answer to a fish enthusiast's problem of disposing nutrient rich water and a hydroponic grower's need for nutrient rich water.

Benefits of Growing Fish and Plants Together

Now why would anyone be interested in aquaponics? Here are the top reasons why:

- Aquaponics is very flexible. There are various sizes and designs that can be built in your backyard, in a greenhouse or even in your home or apartment.

- The fish in an aquaponics system provide a truly organic, natural form of nutrients for plant life.

- There is no need to add fertilizers or to cultivate the soil.

- There is no need for weeding.

- There is no need to water the plants. An aquaponics system uses 2% of the water that a traditional garden does.

- By eliminating the soil in vegetable production, you eliminate all soil borne diseases and do not have to add toxic pesticides.

- If your climate permits or if you are growing indoors or in a greenhouse, you can grow crops year-round.

- A small aquaponics system can produce 100 lbs (45 kg) of fresh fish and yield 200 lbs (90 kg) of fruits and vegetables for consumption or sale every 6 months.

- An aquaponics garden can provide a self sustaining food supply for your family or be scaled up to operate as a profitable small business.

No one is too old or too inexperienced to start their own aquaponics system. If the desire to be self-sufficient is there and you have a passion for raising fish or gardening, aquaponics is right for you! On a hobby scale, aquaponics is catching on quickly. Many backyard gardeners are setting up systems to grow hundreds of pounds of fish and all the fresh vegetables a family needs.

Chapter 11

Understanding the Nitrogen Cycle

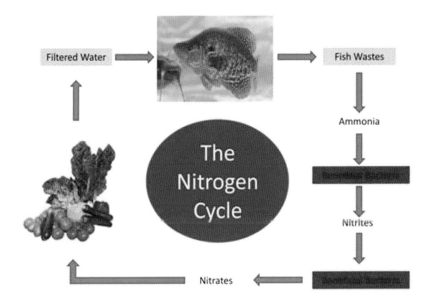

Aquaponics is the practice of raising fish and plants in a closed water system to create a sustainable food supply that takes advantage of the synergistic relationship that exists between these 2 species. The key to an effective aquaponics system is to utilize a natural process called the Nitrogen Cycle to form an ecological system that self maintains the quality and fertility of the water so that both fish and plants prosper.

This involves creating a system that efficiently processes the waste products given off by fish with very little dependence on outside factors such chemicals, water changes and supplemental filters. To do this, the volume of water, rate of circulation, concentration of bacteria, fish load and number of plants in the system must be balanced. Misaligned systems could result in excessive algae, stunted plant growth, fish deaths and create additional work and expense.

In natural habitats, fish populations aren't awfully dense, while in aquaponics, practitioners often attempt to create much bigger concentrations of fish per gallon of water. This can be accomplished through the use of supplemental mechanical and/or chemical purification, however it is preferable from a cost, workload and safety standpoint to balance the system and just allow the natural Nitrogen Cycle to do its work.

When an aquaponics system is initially established, the water is clear and generally free from dangerous substances and bacteria. Once fish are added and begin feeding, the makeup of the water will start to change. As with all living creatures, fish use what nutrients they require from the food and dispose of the rest as waste. This waste decays in the water and develops into ammonia which is toxic to fish. This is when the Nitrogen Cycle kicks in and begins the biological processes which will ultimately take away the ammonia and maintain the quality of the water.

Ammonia is food for certain types of beneficial bacteria. As the ammonia level rises in the aquaponics system, these bacteria form, multiply and consume the ammonia. The fish population, dependent on numbers and size, produce ammonia at different rates and the bacteria population must be able to consume it at the same pace. As the bacteria take in the ammonia, they give off a waste product of their own called nitrites which are also lethal to fish. At that point a second strain of bacteria consumes the nitrites and converts them to nitrates which at moderate levels are not dangerous to aquatic life.

As the system matures, however, the nitrates collect and will eventually reach a problematic level. To maintain, sufficient water quality these nitrates have to be removed from the system and maintained at a level below 50 PPM. In aquaculture, this can be accomplished through frequent water changes which entail a large amount of work, but in aquaponics, this is where the plants come in. Thru the powers of Mother Nature, plants just happen to need nitrogen to grow and they can obtain this necessary element by consuming the nitrates. By removing the nitrates the water is made safe for the fish who continue to feed and emit waste repeating the cycle.

By creating an appropriate balance between the fish and plant populations, water quality can be maintained in an aquaponics system and an abundant harvest of fish and plants can be achieved with the minimum of maintenance effort and cost.

Chapter 12

How to Design an Aquaponics System

While there are many different ways to configure aquaponics systems, there are some standard design principles. For example, most aquaponics designs separate the fish tanks and plant beds. In addition, the fish tanks and the plant beds are located at different elevations in order to take advantage of gravity in circulating the water. The density of the fish and plant populations also need to be kept in balance so you do not either under nourish the plants or pollute the fish tank water. Starting from these basic principles, there are many different variables that can be applied to customize an aquaponics design.

The size of fish tank (250 gallons is the minimum recommendation) determines how much produce can be grown and should be matched to the size of the plant bed. At the most basic level, the fish tank is simply a container to hold water that is safe for raising fish. This container can take the form of a standard aquarium, a backyard pond, or really any "tank" made out of fish safe materials. The water return can be through pipes or more decoratively take the form of a waterfall or stream.

Other variables include the use of supplemental filtration, the location and arrangement of the plumbing to move the water, the type of plant bed and the amount and frequency of water circulation and aeration.

In general, an aquaponics system is an offshoot of well established hydroponic designs that have been adapted to accommodate fish and filtration. The fish tank works like the nutrient reservoirs in hydroponics and the grow beds are similar to grow beds in hydroponics. What follows are descriptions of 2 popular alternatives:

Raft System

In a raft aquaponics system, plants are grown on Styrofoam boards (rafts) that float on top of water. In most cases, this is in a tank separate from the fish tank. Water flows continuously from the fish tank through the raft tank and then back to the fish tank. This is similar to the hydroponics N.F.T. design but the water level in the grow bed is deeper. There is usually some means of mechanical filtration between the 2 tanks to remove bulk debris.

Beneficial bacteria live throughout the aquaponics system, converting fish waste products from ammonia to nitrite and then to nitrate. The nitrates provide nutrients which are consumed by the plants which removes the nitrate filtering the water. The extra water in the plant bed tank also provides a buffer for avoiding potential water quality problems. Most commercial aquaponics systems use some variation of this method, which is well established and highly productive. Hobbyists who are interested in maximizing production also use this design

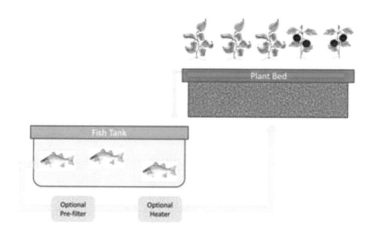

Aquaponics Media Bed Design

Media Bed

In this type of aquaponics system, the plant bed is a tank or container that is filled with gravel, or some other filter media. The plants' roots are embedded in the gravel and the water either runs continuously or the bed is periodically flooded from the fish tank. The filtered water then drains back to the fish tank. The continuous method is preferred if you are using a decorative display such as a waterfall to return water to a backyard fish pond. The flood and drain method will save electricity, water loss and operating hours on the pump and is the same as the Ebb and Flow method in hydroponics except that the fish provide the nutrients. The Media Bed design is simple to operate and build. It is used by most hobbyists who operate an aquaponics system in their backyard. Beneficial bacteria reside in the filter material and all waste, including solids, is broken down within the plant bed. Supplemental mechanical filtration can be added but is not required. This type of aquaponics system involves fewer components and is simpler to build and operate but the output of food per square foot is much lower than the raft system.

Chapter 13

Aquaponics Design Criteria

Aquaponics is a relatively new practice and various types of aquaponics plans are still developing. So far 2 primary designs have evolved. First, there is the raft system where the plants are grown on polystyrene boards that float on top of the water with continuous water flow. Secondly, there is the media bed system, which uses gravel, lava rock or another filtration substance for the plant bed. In the media bed system, the pump cycles on and off, alternatively flooding the plant bed and then utilizing gravity to drain the water back into the fish tank. The arrangement and size of the system is ultimately by the type and scale of food production that is required, the space available and the expertise of the practitioner.

Relative Component Size

Most raft systems utilize three components, fish tanks, plant beds and filtration devices. The relative size of the fish and plant components can be as simple as maintaining a 1 to 1 ratio of water volume, but research has shown that the surface area of the plant beds can be as high as 7 times the surface area of the fish tanks and carry 75% of the water volume. One of the advantages of the raft system is that the high volume of water carried in the multiple tanks provides a buffer that enables a high density of fish to be safely stocked and subsequently harvested. With a raft system, at harvest, the tank can carry up to 0.5 lbs of fish per gallon while safely maintaining water quality. Most commercial aquaponics operations use this method.

The aggregate bed in a media system can provide sufficient filtration so only 2 components are required. The ratio between these components is safely designed at a 1 to 1 surface area ratio, but the plant bed can go as high as 2 or 3 times the size of the fish tank. Due to the use of filter media instead of water in the grow beds, the safe stocking ratio is less than the raft system and equals 0.2 lbs of fish per gallon at harvest. This means if the species of fish you are raising weigh 2 lbs at maturity you can stock 25 fish in a 250 gallon tank. The media system is generally simpler and less expensive to set up and operate and is used by most hobbyists but in terms of production, it is less efficient than the raft system. Using these guidelines for planning purposes, the size of an aquaponics system can be calculated for different levels of desired food production.

Aquaponics Design Based on Fish Yield

The most popular fish used in aquaponics are tilapia. Tilapia can typically grow from fingerlings to 1 lb in 5 to 6 months, so 2 harvests of eatable size fish can be produced per year. Using these planning numbers, a 250 gallon fish tank with a harvest ratio of .2 lbs per gallon can produce about 100 lbs of fish per year. A 1000 gallon tank or four 250 gallon tanks can produce 400 lbs of fish.

Aquaponics Design Based on Produce Yield

The aquaponics method, the type of fish, the density of the population, the feeding rate, and water flow rate must all be considered when determining the actual size of the plant bed that can be supported by various size fish tanks but a general rule of thumb is 1 to 2 ft of growing area for every 10 gallons of water. Using this ratio a 250 gallon tank can support a grow bed of up to 50 sq ft. A plant bed this size can produce around 300 lbs of tomatoes, 600 lbs of lettuce or 100 lbs of eggplant per year.

Again many other factors effect actual production, but when devising your aquaponics design these factors and ratios can be used to provide a rough sense for the yield of produce and fish that can be expected in a given space.

Aquaponics Design Criteria for a Media Bed System

Here are the recommended guidelines for designing and operating an aquaponics media bed system:

- **Fish Tank Size**

A minimum fish tank size of 250 gallons is recommended. The larger the better since greater volumes allow more room for error because changes in water composition will occur more slowly.

- **Fish Stocking Level**

A mature weight of 1 lb of fish for every 5 gallons of water can be safely maintained in most situations. Harvest the fish as they grow and the density approaches this limit.

- **Grow Bed Size**

Each pound of fish can support 1 sq ft of planting surface area. The grown bed should be 1 ft deep and filled with gravel or a similar aggregate media to anchor the plants and provide a means of mechanical filtration. Plants can be spaced at about 2 times the density of a regular garden.

- ## System Configuration

Grow beds should be positioned above the fish tank. Use a pump to circulate the water from the fish tank flooding the grow bed and use gravity to drain the water from the grow bed back into the tank

- ## System Operation

Run the pump for 15 minutes every hour with a 45 minute drain cycle. Size the pump to circulate the entire volume of water every hour. So the pump capacity should be 4 times the water volume.

Here is an example of applying the aquaponics design criteria:

- Lets assume a 500 gallon fish tank which then can support a density of 100 lbs of fish.

- This volume of fish will produce enough waste to feed 100 sq ft of grow bed surface area or a 10 ft by 10 ft space for planting.

- In this example the water pump should have a capacity of at least 2000 gallons per hour.

As you gain experience these ratios can be adjusted to optimize the yield given your specific set of circumstances, such as types of fish or plants you are raising, indoor or outdoor systems, available lighting and ambient temperature.

- Chapter 14 –

Aquaponics Fish

In selecting aquatic livestock for an aquaponics system there are several key factors that needs to be considered:

- Are the fish being raised primarily for eating or are they ornamental fish that are intended as pets?

- Which type of fish are best suited to the weather, temperature, and general conditions of your location?

- If you are to mixing a variety of fish in a single tank, are these species compatible?

- Fish do not develop or grow identically. Some fish grow faster than others, and larger fish will often bully or even eat smaller fish even though they may be compatible when they are similar size.

- Certain types of freshwater fish are better suited for living in a closed-tank environment and some will not even reproduce at all in holding tanks. If you select those fish, you will have to buy additional fingerlings after a harvest in order to begin the cycle anew.

What follows are the characteristics of some of the most popular fish that are stocked in aquaponic systems:

Edible Fish

Tilapia

Tilapia farming is a popular practice in aquaculture because of their large size, and palatability. Like other large fish, they are a good source of protein and are also among the easiest and most profitable fish to farm. This is due to their omnivorous diet that allows them to dine on the aquatic vegetation that grows naturally in the tank reducing feeding costs. They also tolerate a high stocking density and have a rapid rate of growth (6 to 7 months to harvest size). So tilapia farming can produce two harvests per year, each with a very efficient yield of lbs of fish per volume of water.

Tilapia or as they are also known, St. Peter's fish, are a spiny-finned freshwater fish of the Cichlid family, native largely to Africa and Middle

East. Tilapia are categorized as an invasive species, which means that you have to be extra careful not to accidentally release them into the wild where they can negatively impact the growth and reproduction of native species. Tilapias raised in inland tanks or channels are considered safe for the environment, since their waste and disease is contained.

Tilapia is a mild-flavored freshwater fish that will survive and thrive in holding tanks a consistent water temperature is maintained. The preferred water temperature for optimal growth and reproduction is 82°-86° F. Growth drops off significantly below 68° degrees and the fish will not survive below 50° F.

Tilapia can be raised with a wide variety of other aquatic animals including catfish and prawns. It's mild "non-fishy" taste makes it the 5th most consumed fish in the US. Tilapia farming as part of an aquaponics system can produce a sustainable and balanced food supply for any family and when scaled to a sufficient size can also be a profitable business.

White Bass

White bass are a small member of the bass family usually not weighing more than three to four pounds. Also known as Sandies, these fish also have a short lifespan of only three to four year and grow rapidly to maturity. White bass are temperature tolerant and can be raised in tanks with other fish of a similar or larger size.

White bass are also an excellent tasting fish and unlike tilapia, white bass are carnivorous and can feed easily on small crabs and fish.

Crappies

Crappies have delicious, flaky, white flesh that has earned them the reputation as one of the finest tasting freshwater fish. The Cajun name for crappie in Southern Louisiana, "sac-a-lait," literally translates as "sack of milk," and is a testament to its excellent white meat.

Crappies are prolific breeders and adapt well to closed systems. Unfortunately, crappies need at least two years before they are able to mate and reproduce which can extend the time for the initial harvest. The average size of the adult crappie is between one half and one pound, though they are known to grow much larger.

Carnivorous by nature, crappies should be fed insects and small fish if they are kept in a closed system fish tank or pond. Like the white bass, they can be raised with other fish as long as relative size is considered.

Ornamental Fish

Koi

Koi are a colorful, domesticated version of the common wild carp, Cyprinus Carpio. They can grow to over 3 feet in length and life spans of over 20 years are not uncommon. In Japan, where it is the national fish, koi are family pets and are often given as gifts to acquaintances with backyard ponds.

Koi are omnivores that eat both animal and vegetable food. A good diet for pond fish constitutes both these matters and there are commercial foods are available that provide a wide variety of both. Koi will recognize their owners as they approach the pond at feeding time and will throng to the area where they are normally fed. As large fish that love eating, koi can be trained to eat from the owner's hand. Koi have very distinctive colors and physical characteristics that enable individual fish to be easily recognized. Koi will reproduce in either a fish tank or pond

Goldfish

Goldfish are a relatively small domesticated member of the carp family. Goldfish breeds vary greatly in size, body shape, fin configuration and coloration. Goldfish will reproduce in a fish tank or pond and can survive at a wide range of temperatures. Goldfish are a good choice for very small aquaponic systems since they are hardy and can live in relatively restricted spaces.

Other species of freshwater fish that can power aquaponic systems are:

- Largemouth Bass

- Small Mouth Bass

- Catfish

- Walleye

- Trout

- Crayfish

- Prawns

Chapter 15

Grow Lights

In addition to the proper balance of nutrients, water and air, the correct amount of lighting is the final factor that is needed for soil less gardening to be successful. If your hydroponics, aeroponics or aquaponics garden is outdoors or in a greenhouse, it needs at least 4-6 hours of direct sun; plus 10 more hours of bright light. For inside gardens, you need to duplicate outdoor lighting so plan on 14-16 hours of bright artificial light, followed by 8-10 hours of darkness. Plants need time in the dark time to metabolize and rest.

For plants to flourish, indoor gardens need both the proper concentration of light and light with specific wavelengths. So in choosing lighting systems consider the intensity of output as well as the spectrum of the bulb.

Light intensity is measured by lumens which are the brightness of 1 candle, 1 foot away from the plants. It is estimated that an indoor garden requires about 2000 lumens per square foot for satisfactory plant growth. Spectrum refers to the variety of colors by frequencies that compose light waves. Plants require red/orange light for budding and flowering as well as blue/green wavelengths for growing plant mass.

Standard incandescent bulbs provide a good light intensity and lots of red spectrum light but most of the output is wasted through generated heat. It is definitely not a good choice for an indoor garden and standard fluorescent bulbs are not much better though cooler and cheaper to run.

However, special 'grow' type fluorescent bulbs can produce a satisfactory result. Fluorescent warm, white bulbs provide a good source of red light while the cool white bulbs produce good blue light output. The best approach would be to grow plants to maturity with a cool white fluorescent bulb and later replace it with a warm white bulb for flowering. A simpler but more costly alternative would be to use both types of bulbs at the same time. Fluorescent light are relatively inexpensive to purchase and do not through off much heat. The major disadvantage of fluorescents is that light intensity falls off quickly as the distance from the bulb increases. To really be effective a fluorescent system would have to stay only a few inches from the top of the plant and be moved up as the plant grows.

A second alternative is the use of metal halide or high pressure sodium lighting. These lights are more expensive to purchase than fluorescent bulbs and give off a lot of heat which sometimes requires the use of supplemental ventilation or air conditioning. Both metal halide and high pressure sodium lights produce an extremely high output of illumination in a mixed spectrum making them ideal for an indoor garden. Metal halide is more in the 'blue' range so it works better with plants where healthy leafy growth is the priority while high pressure sodium is more in the 'red' and works better with flowering plants.

The last lighting option for indoor gardening was developed for use on the space station. LED lights, short for "light emitter diodes" are very effective and should eventually dominate the indoor grow light market. These lights emit a broad spectrum in wave length and produce little heat for the amount of light produced. LED lamps are also consume about 70% less electricity than incandescent lights and last 10X as long. The major drawback of LED lighting is the very high initial purchase price. But over the time this is more than made up by savings in electricity and reduced replacement costs. As the technology advances and they become more commonly used the purchase price of LEDs are dropping rapidly.

About the Author

Bob Long was born in the Bronx, NY and grew up in a close-knit blue collar family. His education and work experience is in engineering, as a senior executive at Fortune 500 companies and a small business owner. He has worked in a variety of industries including transportation, finance, healthcare and technology. He has many interests including fishing, gardening, sports and surfing the Internet.

He likes to write about subjects where he has a passionate interest and can draw on his experience as an engineer, businessman and outdoors-man. He currently lives in Texas with his wife of 25+ years, 2 teen age children and bunch of dogs.

Other Books by Bob Long

The EZ Guide To Landscape Lighting

The EZ Guide To Building A Koi Pond

The EZ Guide To Dog Breeds

Printed in Great Britain
by Amazon.co.uk, Ltd.,
Marston Gate.